Copyright © 2022 Nelson Sartoris

Printed in the United States of America

Released by ArsPoetica, an imprint of
Pisgah Press, LLC

Cover image and author caricature by Bill LaRocque
Book layout by A.D. Reed
www.pisgahpress.com

All rights reserved. No portion of this book may be reproduced, stored in a retrieval system, or transmitted in any form or by any means – electronic, mechanical, photocopy, recording, scanning, or other – except for brief quotations in critical reviews or articles, without the prior written permission of the author.

Library of Congress Control Number: 2022942784
Library of Congress Cataloging-in-Publication Data
Sartoris, Nelson/Poetry

ISBN: 9781942016717

First Print Edition August 2022

Unsent Postcards

poems by
Nelson Sartoris

Unsent Postcards

When I was growing up in Chicago in the 1940s and '50s, my family didn't travel often. Vacations cost money, something in short supply. A few years after the War my parents got their first car, a black 1939 Chevy. It took us on short family ventures to the Wisconsin Dells, Niagara Falls, and the Smoky Mountains, the only vacations we took during all those years. We sent postcards to family and friends. Mailing cost: a penny.

Friends, neighbors, and relatives, however, traveled extensively and they sent back many postcards. Most with alluring pastel images of exotic places I hungered to see myself. The back of a postcard had just enough room for an address and brief cliché: having a wonderful time, wish you were here, greetings from California, beautiful scenery, the weather is fantastic.

As a kid I saved them, stored them in a shoebox. Occasionally I'd flip through them and imagine myself reveling in those faraway places. Those postcards were the spark that lit the flame of travel in me that thus far has taken me to 49 states and 24 countries on three continents. I quickly discovered that postcards didn't allow room to discuss the emotional and reflective aspects of travel: what it does and doesn't do for one's soul. Nor were they adequate to attest to odysseys of the mind instead of just physical travels. As Harry Chapin put it in song, "You can travel on for ten thousand miles, and still stay where you are."

Few people send postcards anymore. They text or email or post their photos on Facebook or Instagram. But the sentiments expressed and shared remain the same.

The poems in this book represent unsent postcards from outward, inward, and chimeric journeys of my life, and, regretfully, some not taken. Travel along with me.

Dedication

This book is dedicated to Mike Ross and Bill Petz, two talented poets and gifted poetry instructors who ignited my pen and continue to inspire and encourage me.

Acknowledgments

This book owes its existence to many muses, gifted instructors, fellow poets, and literary friends at the Osher Lifelong Learning Institute at the University of North Carolina Asheville. Many of the poems in this volume were written during the COVID-19 pandemic for a group of 15 poets called the Barricaded Bards. Each week, a member of the group would select a topic, and every member would email their poem to the others for constructive criticism. To those Barricaded Bards (Victoria Bender, Carol Booth, Karen Depew, Kay Duncan, Kim Hayes, Richard Horvath, Jay Jacoby, Ann Karson, Tom Milroy, Bill Petz, Sara Scott, Judy Upjohn, Elizabeth Wallace, Wendy Wieber) I am eternally grateful for not only their poetic advice, but their friendship and camaraderie that helped sustain me through the height of the pandemic.

In other OLLI poetry-writing classes and groups, several addition poets cheerfully engaged in the process of improving each other's poetry. For their individual talent, helpful suggestions, and friendly encouragement I am also indebted. My thanks to all of them: Paula Bannasch, Wallace Bohanon, Eloise Bradham, Jim Carillon, David Castel, Karin Eckert, Lottie Erikson, Roger Munch, Mike Ross, John Ryder, Paul (Schepp) Scheberle, Michael Smith, Mary Vinson, Joan Weiner, Roxanne Zusmer. All have had a hand in shaping and improving some poems in this book. These superb poets, artists and wordsmiths continue to both energize and humble me. I am honored and blessed to be in their company.

I am also indebted to my erudite editor and publisher, Andy Reed, of Pisgah Press, whose keen eye, polished word skills, and friendship made this book possible.

TABLE OF CONTENTS

Unsent Postcards v
Dedication vi
Acknowledgments vii

It's in the Mail

Legacy? 5
Contact 6
Ghostwriter 7
Writing Poems for People Who Don't Like Poetry 8
Small talk 9
Poetry in Motion 10
New Agenda 11
22 Steps 12
Ode for Joy 13
Consonance 14

Sending My Love

Shared Rain 17
Awareness 18
Unveiled 19
Stud* 20
The Chase 21
Touched 22
Transition 23
Then 24
Intimacy 25
Silly Love Poems 26

The Weather Has Changed

A Winter Tale 29
Annual Kaleidoscope 30
Anthropocene Chicxulub 31
COVID Winter 32
At the Margins 33
Early August 34

*Poems that have appeared in previous books by the author

38°C in Verkhoyansk	35
Rain Plans	36
Total Wreck	37
Life Winds	38
Elementary	39
H$_2$O	40
Wind Fall	41
Gone	42
Then One Morning	43
Watchful	44
Where Now?	45

Wish You Were Here

Lone Candle	49
Healing	50
Still Life*	51
Capsized	52
Chased or Chaste	53
Unconditional	54
New Acquaintance	55
Checkout	56
Left Behind	57
When Thinking About Her Again	58
Meet Me Somewhere	59
Missing Memories	60
Agéd Yearnings	61

Scenery is Beautiful

Woodland Wings	65
Uncloaked	66
Quiet	67
A Bird Watching	68
Striptease	69
For the Birds	70
Life Cycle	71
Juggling Jaws	72

Skyward	73
Flight Envy	74
Weep for the Willow	75
I and Thou	76
Eruption	77
Goose Talk	78

Having a Terrible Time

No Vacancy*	81
The Fall	82
Last Night	83
On a Scale of 1 to 10	84
Manhood in America	85
The Hunt	86
Patriotism	87
Melting Pot	88
Kids in the Backseat	90
Dissonance	91
Gaps	92
Ennui	94
White Picket Fences	95
Frenzy	96
Infernal Combustion	97

The Food Is Fantastic

Garnish	101
Tastes Extraordinaire	102
Raw Truth	104
That First Delicious Apple	105
Menu Guide*	106
Rafter Disaster	107
Day Break	108

Lost in Nowhere

Quest	111
Upside Down	112
Drawing Horses	113

At the End of the Day 114
Carnival of Life 115
Close Quarters 116
Day Lily 117
Watering Hole 118
Human Enigma 119
No U-turn 120
Unlike Today 121
Interruptions 122
Internal Dialogue 123
Evolving Invocation 124
Bonding 125
Ode to the Double Helix 126
It's Official 127
A Past Future 128
At the Market 129
Dust 130
Dimmer 131

Never Coming Back Here

American Relapse 135
Dotage 136
End Times 137
Pronouns 138
Final Renaissance 139
Nearer 140
Never Again 141
Unmasked 142
More to Lose 143
Poetry Journal 144
Widower 145
Stigmata 146
Deception 147
Surrogates 148
Memory Shackles 149
Ninth Decade 150

Greetings from Yesterday

Mature Meanings	153
Yesterday's Sundays	154
Way of the World	155
A Dollar. A Day	156
Benchmarks*	157
Ancient Paths	158
Indelible Ink	159
Dark Spot	160
Putting It to Rest	161
Regrettable	162
Rural Sanctuaries	163
FOMO	164
Top 40 Countdown	165
Shotgun	166
X-Rated	167
The American Game	168
Inside My Book's Cover	169
Babel Babble	170

There's No Place Like Home

Curious Appellation	173
All Fixed	174
Hanging Out	175
Mobile Home	176
Monday Joy	177
Stuff	178
Summer Symphony	179
My Father's Heir Apparent	180
Water Is Only Good for Washing Your Feet	181
Collateral Damage	182
Unrelated	183
Special Delivery	184
Fledging	185
Liquid Memories	186
Misconception	188
About the Author	190

Unsent Postcards

Nelson Sartoris

Nelson Sartoris

Nelson Sartoris

LEGACY?

Patience may be a virtue
but it isn't one of mine,
had more of it when younger
now I'm running out of time.

Urgent need to write something
that I think ought to matter.
important or illusion?
most likely it's the latter.

Still I write all through the night
poems to serve as legacy,
but if no one opts to read them
poetry's still cheap therapy.

Contact

brush meets canvas
chisel meets stone
bow meets string
pen meets paper
ballet slippers meet floor
fingers meet wet clay

in these moments of contact
our potential is revealed
we become human

GHOSTWRITER

you rest your head on my down feathers
yet presume dreamy thoughts arise from within you

you hear my songs in the background
yet think rhythm and rhyme originate in your voice

you notice my colors flash by your eyes
yet imagine vibrant images emerge from your palette

you observe my wing beats as I rise on the wind
yet assume it is your own words and verse that soar

you dip my quill in your ink well
and believe you have written the poem

Nelson Sartoris

WRITING POEMS FOR PEOPLE WHO DON'T LIKE POETRY

Best to keep it short
or else you will thwart
the readers you court

Don't be too subtle
otherwise what'll
come is rebuttal

Use mostly simple words
or you'll turn off two-thirds
who think poetry's absurd

Forced rhyme is a crime
you don't need to rhyme
every line all the time

Don't write about a topic
that's too kaleidoscopic
nor one that's too myopic

Instead choose a subject
upon which they'll reflect
so their souls can connect

Try to make it pithy
and a wee bit witty
perhaps a wry ditty

Always end with a twist
give readers the same bliss
as if smacked with a kiss

Then they'll crave another poem
won't think of them as dumb
poetry no longer loathsome

SMALL TALK

On the way to the mailbox today
the roses along the walk spoke to me.
I stopped to listen,

With all these fallen colored leaves around
we're feeling fragile and old. We're fearful
of the coming cold.

I tried to comfort them, *Death is not
to be feared, you and your progeny
will be resurrected in the spring.*

They thanked me, but were still dismayed,
didn't tell them I was also. I just said,
I'll mulch your roots and trim you before winter comes.

My dog observed me talking with the roses,
he looked at me sensing something was wrong.
I shared with him the roses' concerns and upcoming plight.

Told him, *It makes me sad. I will miss them.*
He nodded and said, *I understand. I'll try
to comfort you through the winter in their stead.*

That's so thoughtful, I said, *you're such a good boy.*
He replied, *When I tell the cat she probably won't understand,
you know she's not very fond of the roses.*

I tried to reassure him, *Don't worry, I'll talk to her.*

POETRY IN MOTION

born a soul who can't idly sit
repose alien to this poet

but at the wheel my mind's replete
all is bliss in the driver's seat

gear up, gear down, go fast, go slow
contentment comes synced in tempo

engine purrs, thoughts accelerate
driving alone, concepts gestate

traversing miles, verse seeds are sown
born to go somewhere yet unknown

fresh fertile vistas soon abound
over each hill, every curve around

paying heed to just words and road
poems in my head flow and unfold

roll north, roll south, roll east, roll west
muse spews free, lines, rhymes manifest

all is fine behind the windshield
turn the wheel, poetry's revealed

NEW AGENDA

Two years of COVID
   of masks
   of anxiety
   of isolation
a long two years...

Would that I were free of this threat—
I might sit at a favorite bar
   with friends and a beer.
I could shop for things
   somewhere not Amazon.
I might fly high above to a sandy beach
   where the sun shines every day.
I could dine with family
   at a favorite restaurant.
I could attend a first-run movie,
   theater popcorn in hand.

But more likely I'd just be sitting here
writing a different poem,
anxious to share it
with poet friends—

in person.

Nelson Sartoris

Twenty-Two Steps

Anticipation heightens as I approach.
What awaits may have traveled
thousands of miles to land in my hands
twenty-two steps from my front door.

Along my short march to the mailbox
        denuded rose plants urge me to stop
        and attend to an early spring trim,
through gelid soil hyacinths peek
        and push imploring me to pause
        and witness their miracle rebirth,
the neighbor's dog, tongue out,
        tail in wag mode, looks at me longingly
        in hope of a rub behind her ears,
fetal dogwood buds beckon me
        to marvel as their winter wombs
        whisper imminent dilation,
in the bare oak a mockingbird
        beseeches me to wait and listen as he
        practices his upcoming courting song,
a frisky gray squirrel invites me
        to share his joy in uncovering
        last fall's buried bounty.

But I ignore all these callings. I'm on a mission,
I am singularly focused on what might be in the box.
I hasten the last few steps, eager
as a prospector approaching a motherlode.
I pull down the lid and reach for the prize --
but alas, once again, no surprise, just another bill
and an ad for a sale.

Retracing my steps from the inert black metal box
of disappointment, the ignored flora and fauna
mock my foolish disregard with a scoffing
reminder to reorder my priorities.

ODE FOR JOY

Done are duties of the day,
quiet finally arrives,
relief from dissonant
noises in my head.
Time to uncork random
elixir of thoughts,
a moment to distill
chaos into clarity.

Windows open
for ideas to become words,
blank page intimidates,
yet invites.
Paralysis at first, then a word,
then another, no destination
yet in sight, I'm driving
at night without headlights.

Time and the world disappear.
Some days lines roll down
my sleeve onto the page.
Through some enigmatic process
a rough draft appears,
much work still to do --
edit, delete, rearrange,
refine before bottling.

All that can wait, must wait
to ripen, ferment, mature,
time now to mull it over
with a dram of aged single malt,
a moment of joy and serenity
in an otherwise ordinary day.
I sip slowly,
word by word.

Nelson Sartoris

Consonance

Conditions must be perfect
for water vapor to crystallize on trees—
temperature below freezing,
calm winds, freezing fog
create enchanting mystical ice called rime.

Words must be perfect
for lines to coalesce into poem on paper—
harmonious sounds,
rhythm and meter in sync
create enchanting mystical verse called rhyme.

Postcard

Sending my love

Place stamp here

Nelson Sartoris

SHARED RAIN

Soft rain outside my open window
wakes me before dawn.
I lie alone wondering if the rain has
wakened you and you are thinking of me.

Does the fresh damp also kiss your face,
is the smell of sweet air as soothing to you,
do you hear gentle drops caress tree leaves,
does the slight cool breeze also heighten
rather than ease your passions?

Strange how you feel near when you are not,
strange how longing stirs the soul almost
as much as your presence, stranger still
the feeling you are feeling the same
sublime bliss of shared rain.

Awareness

It happened
when I discovered I could see clearer in the dark,
when there was no blinding sunshine
to illuminate worldly things to distract me,
my vision most acute when there was nothing to see,
when the essence of my sentience was bare.

It happened
when I realized I could hear better
if there was only silence,
when serene music emerged only from within,
when the din of external audio insults
didn't muffle clarity of mind.

It happened
when I sensed I could savor
imagined food aromas and tastes
without meals on the table,
when that savoring was more
satisfying than eating.

It happened
when I learned I could touch
the shrouded stories of my life
when there was nothing else to touch,
when no tactile sensation
disturbed the present.

It happened
when I could sense your presence
by the gentle aura of your being.

UNVEILED

He'd never seen it before
but knew it was there.
All that was visible
had been grief and despair.

A dram of scotch,
their shared preferred fare.
A few swings in a chair
buoys this cautious old pair.

An invite to share
moments in her lair,
a close hug of great care
leaves both floating on air.

hardly an affair,
more like a prayer
for two lives to repair
in a way that they dare.

And then with a flair
she tossed back her hair,
gave him a young smile
long hidden in nightmare.

STUD

On the lush green
the old stallion grazes lazily,
but he is not content,
his days of stud now history.

Across the plain he spies
young fillies, their manes flowing,
haunches fresh, gams shapely,
bodies toned, lean, glowing.

Memories of the chase
race through his colt brain,
temptation in his heart
pulses in his veins.

He could catch them still, he thinks,
they may feign hard-to-win,
but would toss their tails,
rein their pace, welcome him.

He struggles to recall
what to do if one calls his bluff.
Then a silvery mare sidles up to him,
shares the rich green—it is enough.

THE CHASE

He had thought the catch everything
but it was always the chase,
the thrill pursuing a wild filly,
her tousled feral hair flowing
as she tried to outrun him,
her tail a frenzied comet,
her lathered coat glistening,
her eyes fierce with freedom,
her hooves barely touching ground
flaying dry earth in their wake.

Exhilaration of the chase was seminal.
The old stallion knows this now.
Memories of pursued sunlit manes
race across his mind,
his heart pounds with virile fire.
Oh, to be young and swift again!

One last chase might still be his,
if only that frisky gray mare
would slow her pace. It matters less
what happens when he catches her,
the chase would be victory enough.
Yes, it had always been the chase.

TOUCHED

Only one feeling
transcends the blissful moment
of touching her skin,
>   the response of her touched skin
>   answering back to my hand

TRANSITION

    Grief etched deeply in her facial rifts
that only long forgotten smiles might erase
Age worn like an overly-large overcoat
smothering any vestiges of youthful spirit
    Motions slowed by weight of hopelessness
as if leaden steps could delay life from slipping away

    Yet an ember of yearning in her eyes
can still be seen by those caring enough to look
But how can she latch onto hope, reboard life's train
when all the stations are unfamiliar and remote
And how to begin this journey alone, how to
find a close companion, how to let him find her

    Then by accident she stumbles into his life
wary and cautious she takes baby-steps toward trust
    The closer she allows him, the younger she feels
darkness and pain slowly eclipsed by smiles and laughter
    Closer still and her eyes reveal the caring light
nestled in youthful glow of renewed desire

    She slowly stirs alive again, ready for more life, for love
but she rides an unfamiliar train on a foreign track
    She knows not where or how fast this train is going
nor how long the ride, it just feels good to have a ticket
    But how to know when transition ends and she's arrived,
the ride, smiles, soft moments perhaps the only destinations

Nelson Sartoris

THEN

I was a stream without water
tree without bark,
lyrics without melody
bone without flesh
bird without wings
poem without words
air without oxygen
an empty ocean
then . . . you

INTIMACY

Obvious now,
that once mysterious essence of intimacy.
Long believed to lie in eye-to-eye contact,
a locked gaze that connected, welded two people.
Important, yes, but not enough.

If not engaged looks, then certainly touch,
that divine experience of hand on skin,
skin on skin. Deception difficult to hide
in a touch and reciprocal skin response.
Important, true, but touch can be sensuous
without being intimate.

Perhaps intimacy is grounded in words,
eloquent protestations and vows.
But even poor poets can lie, deceive.

It's not words, touch, locked eyes,
but soft quiet tone of voice
that conveys and betrays the soul's truth.

Intimacy is not in the words spoken,
but in how they are spoken. Trust comes from
the tongue of tonal truth. It's the heart's tone
the soul hears, understands, believes.

Silly Love Poems

"You'd think people would've had enough of silly love
　　poems,
I look around me, and I see it isn't so."*

But can love be as serene as love poems portray?
Are the passions of the soul capable of the magic
　　embedded in beguiling words?
Is the intimacy portrayed ever as harmonious
　　as the perfect rhymes?
Can the allure of soft flesh compare to a rosebud
　　embellished by seductive verse?

Or are love poems just a ruse, a come-on, a con-job
　　to make our love lives seem inadequate,
　　not up to snuff, our partners deficient?
Tell us true, Shelley, Shakespeare, Browning,
　　were your loves as fine as your poems?

"I need to know, 'cause here I go again."*

*Apologies to Paul McCartney

Postcard

The weather has changed

Place stamp here

Nelson Sartoris

A Winter Tale

I watch as snow-laden dusk
enshrouds my feeder,
a biting north wind propels
heavy flakes ever more horizontal.

A solitary male bluebird snatches
a few final safflower seeds,
nourishment that must sustain him
for fifteen hours of bitter cold darkness.

His mate lost to a Cooper's Hawk
during final warm days of fall,
he faces this endless night alone,
armed only with energy from these seeds

and promise of morning light.
I wonder where he will seek shelter,
perhaps a leeward hollow in tree bark,
or nestled in a brush pile,

maybe a recess in the eaves
of the old shed. I worry he won't survive
this frozen night to court
a new mate come spring.

I wish I could invite him in,
here in the warmth of this lonely house
to share heartbreaks of loss,
he might help me make it through the night.

Annual Kaleidoscope

white slowly gives way to brown
in gray backgrounds

silvery rain and golden light birth
fresh verdant hues
a tapestry of spring greenery
      lime braided with jade
      mint quilted with sage
      olive woven with emerald

all meld into middling summer green
before chromatic blossoms erupt
in kaleidoscopic spectacle
on backdrops of blue

chlorophyll-exhausted leaves
ignite into red, yellow, orange flames
which morph to brown and gray again
awaiting white

Anthropocene Chicxulub

No need to wait
for a large asteroid
this time

We future dinosaurs
are doing the job
all by ourselves

COVID WINTER

night seems to arrive just after day has begun,
darkness the unwelcome visitor who never leaves,
truant emergence of coveted morning glow,
just cold gunmetal gray.

phantom sun, when seen, seems glued to the horizon,
endless daily cycles unravel in this winter of COVID,
warding off depression from futile stasis
the only meaningful labor of the day.

theater, dining with friends, hugs, maskless smiles
now taboo -- human interaction, once a necessity,
has itself become a lethal virus.
survival alone now the only reason to survive.

AT THE MARGINS

easy to understand fog and mist
and totally overcast skies,
just simple aerosols,
visible water micro-droplets,
moisture-saturated air cooled to its dew point.

cumulous clouds, however,
are defined by their margins,
the mysterious abrupt contrast
between white and blue.

the severe border between
visible water droplets and clear sky
is the miracle, the moisture gradient
too gradual for sharp edges,
keen margins shouldn't exist,

but they do.

Early August

already her leaves are tired

exhausted from the early spring rush
to garner light
to birth delicate white blossoms
before the emerging canopy
absorbed all the sun

star of the forest floor in April,
she now languishes under taller,
broader brethren,
all but unnoticed
in early August
save for her fatigued foliage

38°C IN VERKHOYANSK

Adam's invisible hand
blessed grabs for the green
consequences unseen.

They dug for bituminous lodes
steam engines rolled
wallets overflowed.

Drilled for black gold
internally combusted
dividends manifold.

Fracked for methane
burners aflame
large capital gains.

Sixteen billion selfish palms
lined their pockets
with temporal profits.

With Adam's hand invisible
believers thought it biblical
but then came the revelation

of God's garden desecration.
Hell wrought by Adam's greedy scam
we all had a hand in his plan.

The price for being myopic:
Eden's temperature skyrockets
Siberia mimics the tropics.

Rain Plains

with normal now abnormal,
uncertainty the only certainty,

I've got rain plans
to cushion me from life's storms,
I've got rain plans
when troubles become the norm.

I've got rain plans
with a woman I can call my friend,
let what others think be damned,
her longing look a welcome godsend.

I've got rain plans
with a woman who understands,
who makes no demands
love in each touch of her hands.

I've got rain plans,
let storms come, I welcome them,
I've got rain plans
for when my life begins again.

Total Wreck

leaking oil
air conditioning broken
engine warning lights flashing
dirty exhaust
clogged air filter
overheating
defective steering

time to take Earth
into the shop

Life Winds

a small wailing squall
pushes out against the debris
of yesterdays,
insists its voice be heard,
scours its surroundings,
alters the world.

gales and gusts
shape everything it touches
and it in turn is sculpted
by what is touched.

it matures midst intermittent rays
of sunshine
and occasional harrowing storms,
its tempests
inevitably calmed by exhaustion
and resignation.

it winds down into a reflective breeze
then dwindles to a final breath
of moving air
before settling again
into the stillness of dust.

Elementary

before atoms

naïve ancients
believed other substances
were life's essential elements
    Earth, the solid substance of being
    Air, the ethereal vapor of the spirit
    Fire, the infernal energy of transformation
    Water, the liquid elixir of vitality
all things combinations of these fundamentals

modern humans
    poisoners of Earth
    befoulers of Air
    igniters of apocalyptic Fires
    polluter of Waters
defilers of essentials

the ancients knew

H$_2$O

Water is wet,
but one molecule
of water isn't wet.
How many molecules of water
are needed to create wetness?

Steam is hot,
but one molecule
of water above 100°C isn't hot.
How many molecules of water vapor
are needed to create hotness?

Ice is solid, cold,
but one molecule
of water below 0°C isn't solid.
How many molecules of water
are needed to create ice?

Wind Fall

a sudden harsh cold north wind
this bright late fall day
rips tranquility asunder

immediately flakes begin to fall,
large flakes, enormous flakes,
no two alike

in an abrupt blinding blizzard
they dervish to the ground
in frenzied vortices

within minutes they cover
the green of summer past
with blankets of yellow, orange, red

this colorful herald of winter
will not melt, no shovel yet required,
just a rake

GONE

When man is gone from the Earth
will some new species find his bones
conclude his brains were too small?

When man is gone from the Earth
will any future creature
find a use for his guns?

When man is gone from the Earth
what will happen to all
his money?

When man is gone from the Earth
will God, heaven, and hell
still exist?

When man is gone from the Earth
will any species except dogs
not rejoice?

When man is gone from the Earth
will the man in the moon
also disappear?

THEN ONE MORNING

Then one morning they wake
and it is silent—
the sky absent of song,
no darting movements, color gone.

They realize the landscape
is gray, no flowers,
no greenery, no wildlife,
trees naked, only it isn't winter.

They notice the sky
is ochre, the sun dim and hazy,
the air difficult to breathe,
temperature steamy, oppressive.

They see flood waters engulfing
their land, the angry ocean rising,
fresh water reservoirs
full of garbage, drying up.

Turning to the news over coffee
they smile, the stock market
is up again, they are wealthy,
tomorrow they'll be even richer.

photo by Nelson Sartoris

WATCHFUL

Had you been there all summer
hiding in green foliage?
watching me? watching over me?

I only noticed you when leafy camouflage
had been discarded. There you were,
at dusk, peeking under a large branch,
almost spherical face, two tiny remnant leaves
for eyes, wispy nose, perfect lips.

Figment of my imagination? Perhaps,
but I can't unsee you. What are you telling me?
Speak, so this human mind might
understand tree talk.

WHERE NOW?

Where do I go now, Wendell,
when I despair for the world?

Sequoias burned
oceans full of plastic
Blake tygers no longer burning bright
rhinos and pandas confined to zoos
fewer Nash belly-full pelicans
jungles now plantations
Millay Aprils empty of whispers and butterflies

Where do I lie down
when the wood drake cannot be found?

Where do I find peace
when wild things are gone?

Postcard

Wish you were here

Place stamp here

LONE CANDLE

in a world
darkened by disease
deadened by environmental degradation
corrupted by greed
polluted by dishonest power
crippled by hate
hope dims in grim leaden tomorrows

only light visible
promise in her eyes
only bliss tangible
honesty of her touch
only love salient
passion in her heart

HEALING

always being damaged
always striving to heal

cut hand bleeds,
miraculously, blood platelets
rush to the site, stem the flow,
scab begins to form.
bodies know how to heal

foot bone breaks,
miraculously, callus forms
at point of fracture,
new bone cells start to grow.
bodies know how to heal

bacterial infection invades
respiratory system,
miraculously, army of white
blood cells attack invaders.
bodies know how to heal

heart breaks,
but there are no miracles,
no platelets, no callus, no white cells
to mend a wounded heart.
lost love leaves scars that always bleed

STILL LIFE

Not a word is spoken
the entire afternoon.
you are here, reading,
tending to chores, cooking,
content in your own world,
seemingly unaware of my presence.

It's as if I am alone,
yet I'm not lonely,
my life is whole,
full and fulfilled
by your mere existence
within these walls.

But if you weren't present,
separated from me by death
or otherwise departed,
somehow gone
with no prospect of return,
there would be no way of silencing
the silent crescendo
of crushing solitude.

The joy of coming home
replaced by terror
closing the door behind me,
confronted with absolute emptiness,
your absence only amplifying ghosts
of your former presence,
then panic with fear,
frantic in search for purpose living
without you,

alone.

Capsized

You were rife like the ocean
You were all that I could see
You roiled like the ocean
Ebbed slowly away from me

You were rapt like the ocean
With dark depths unknown to me
You lured me to your ocean
Then swam away casually

You were rogue like the ocean
Riptided my soul from me
I drowned in your cruel ocean
Nothing left but sea debris

Chased or Chaste

Opting to remain chaste
is decorum misplaced,
desire is no disgrace
when new love suits your taste.

No need for careless haste,
yet the urge to embrace,
my arms around your waist
both feeling our hearts race . . .

Let not pleasure be erased,
express cravings bold-faced,
if both yearn to be chased
but not caught . . . such a waste.

UNCONDITIONAL

unconditionally
I love the old red oak tree
in my back woods
the oak need not
love me in return

unconditionally
I love the purple hyacinths
harbinger of other spring blossoms
the hyacinths need not
love me in return

unconditionally
I love the sound of thunder
as the storm approaches
the storm need not
love me in return

unconditionally
I love the sunset
the array of colors every evening
the sunset need not
love me in return

unconditionally
I have loved you
in sickness and in health
unaware that under no conditions
would you love me in return

NEW ACQUAINTANCE

This past COVID year
we've seen each other many times,
but have never met.

You seem quite pleasant,
nice smile, easy laugh, bright,
unpretentious, engaging quick wit.

We've often talked in the presence
of others, but never one-on-one
over a cup of coffee.

We are virtual 2D Zoom acquaintances
each lacking the other's
third dimension.

If I were to run into you
on the street today
I may not recognize you.

Your face would be familiar,
but little else. I picture you
well proportioned, short, nimble.

If you are heavy and tall
I might walk right past you,
anticipated body image mistaken.

And perhaps the same for you,
disarmed by my waistline, my slight limp,
the bald spot on the back of my head.

Checkout

I didn't notice her at first, I was just happy for an empty checkout aisle. But after unloading my groceries on the moving belt, there she was. No wonder I missed her—small, frail, elderly, every bit of 85. Her nametag says, "Helen." Her hand tremors complicate her checkout tasks.

Why is she working here? Is her social security so meager she needs the money to subsist? Has her lifelong husband died leaving her at the brink of bankruptcy with staggering medical bills? Has she blown her retirement money on lottery tickets, or used it to aid struggling family members? I'm reluctant to engage her for answers since she has difficulty enough without explaining her situation to me.

Do you want this beer in a bag, Sir? she asks cheerfully. *If you need help, Harold here can help you out to your car.* I realize then, Harold, the bagger, is as old as she is. I wonder, too, why he's here. I give Helen my coupons, insert my credit card, then it registers—as Helen thanks me and wishes me a good day she smiles endearingly at Harold, their eyes lock. He grins back, then winks at me.

LEFT BEHIND

He thought he'd die first.
He was sure of it. He dwindled his closet,
his papers, his tools, his books
so she'd have few things of his to dispose.
He left detailed notes about managing assets,
bills, car maintenance, household issues,
even left a love poem where he knew
she would find it—about why she
should seek happiness with another,
that it would please him if she did.

He was wrong, he's the one left alone.
In the deafening silence, he stares
at her full closet, torn with uncertainty
about whether and how to empty it.
How can he part with that turquoise dress
she'd worn so elegantly at their daughter's wedding,
that comforting gray sweater she'd always
donned on quiet, cold winter evenings,
those silky purple paisley pajamas that lured
his touch through so many nights?

In the corner stands her jewelry chest packed
with memories, gems and precious-metal gifts
bestowed on special occasions and distant travels,
the Chilean lapis bracelet, the gray topaz
pendant from Venice, the Haitian larimar
earrings, the sleek silver Mexican necklace.
What should he do with them? How can he discard
those moments? Yet how can he bear looking daily
at this chest with all those memories inside?

Then, in the bottom drawer—a note!
*Please donate all my things to those who need
and value them, then seek happiness in another—
buy her fresh jewelry befitting her taste—
and silky purple paisley pajamas.*

When Thinking about Her Again

I am a desert thirsty for rain

deaf to the world hoping to recall her laugh
hungry longing for the quiet place of her presence
amused conjuring her facial image in billowing clouds
blissful remembering the delicate touch of her hand

dazed visualizing the vibrant light dancing in her eyes
beguiled dreaming of her hair wafting gently in the wind
mesmerized musing on soft words spoken through her smile
aroused like wildflowers awakening at dawn

I am a desert thirsty for rain

MEET ME SOMEWHERE

somewhere deep in nature
> without
>> anyone around for miles
>> mechanized background noise
>> cellphones
> without judgment of others

somewhere
> where
>> all music is bird song
>> time is forgotten
>> only truth is spoken
> where love is trusted

somewhere
> under a tree
>> lie close to me
>> in Rumi's grass . . .
> we'll eat the whole apple

Missing Memories

Is this the beginning of Alzheimer's?

The inability to recall
cozy evenings nestled by the fire with her
joyful vacation drives to the west coast
her come-hither glances across a crowded room
those starry nights sailing the Mediterranean
spontaneous passionate love-making in the middle of the day
her hand reaching out to mine at a quiet restaurant
intimate moments of soft pillow talk on weekend mornings

These memories escape me, I cannot summon them

Perhaps they never happened

Aged Yearnings

Fog of old age settles in,
a solitary end comes into view,
how and when the only uncertainty.

Immobilized by loneliness, habit, viscid joints,
each day, each night a hopeless
cloistered repetition.

But the heart still beats—
beats for shared stories, for laughter,
eye contact, bread broken together.

Beats for human touch, night warmth
of spoon-nested bodies, loving smiles,
intimate conversation, shared sips of scotch.

Life's end an inevitable lone odyssey
unless one finds bliss with another
whose heart beats with agéd yearnings.

Nelson Sartoris

Postcard

Scenery is beautiful

Place stamp here

WOODLAND WINGS

Into deep woods at dusk,
senses keen, apprehensive,
the night forest foreboding,
I, and my kind, now strangers
where once was home.

In fading light, chickadee acrobats
forage a final feeding, rowdy jays
screech twilight codas,
in deeper darkness a goshawk
carves his way through branch mazes
with lightning speed,
the stealthy barred owl silently glides
through moonlit shadows
in pursuit of prey.

Clumsily stumbling over roots and rocks,
eyes ill-adapted to the night,
songs of light have given way to dark sounds
that both invite and frighten.
Am I tenant or trespasser?

Back against bark, nerves finally calmed,
solace settles,
perhaps by this return to roots
I might emerge at dawn—
with wings.

Nelson Sartoris

photo by Nelson Sartoris

UNCLOAKED

December reveals the skeleton,
scars, lesions, bones of broken limbs,
obtuse angled offshoots from nature's pollarding,
all in sharp focus of winter's defoliated lens.

black-silhouetted against a cold gray sky
its resolute dendritic quest for light exposed,
writhe, skewed branches speak of struggle,
wind, ice and heavy snow thwarted foes.

survival has not been easy, yet
it still stands, proud of its battle history,
defiant in its umbrel bearing,
noble in fleshless asymmetry.

stripped of green sheath embellishments
it unashamedly stands naked in stoic splendor,
a testament to life and hope, uncloaked
of everything -- except its own innate truth.

QUIET

no wind, no rustling leaves, no bird song,
no vehicle noise in the distance,
no lawnmower roar, no insects buzzing,
no hum of neighbors' air conditioners,
no TV audio inanity in the background,
no crinkling of snack bags,
no dogs barking, no human cacophony,
no motorcycle testosterone,
no airplane drone, no music,
nothing

for precious minutes today
a rare confluence of silence

my mind keen with clarity
my heart hesitant to beat
my soul cognizant of its being

quiet—
the beautiful sound
of awareness

A Bird Watching

4:30am:
Why are you up so early, wife asks sleepily.
Going birding.
This early?
Report of a Lawrence warbler sighting sixty miles north of here.
A what?
Very rare hybrid of a Golden-winged and Blue-winged.
Oh—Good luck.

11:00am:
I'm home, dear.
Are you hungry? How about some pancakes?
That would be great.
Well, did you see it?
Saw Goldens and Blues, but no Lawrence,
going again tomorrow. I'm sure he saw me.
Good for him—you are a rare species.

STRIPTEASE

You come on stage slowly
peeking from behind a dark winter curtain,
festooned in budding green dress
you begin to reveal yourself,
never in haste, always with taste,
kindling anticipation and ardor.

In sun's spotlight you expose
a hint of pale flesh,
the fresh pure innocence
of a newborn, a brilliant white
four-petal blossom so pristine,
so ready to burst and excite.

Aroused, we await the climax
of your exotic splendor,
imaginations savor every sensuous step,
we thirst to imbibe every moment,
and finally, there you are
in your delicate grandeur,

As you lure us to lust
you tease us further—with music building
to crescendo you let fall a petal,
then another, then more... but as you
continue to shed alluring raiments,
ecstasy does not escalate, it abates.

Stop!! we plead, don't remove any more,
but you are in a frenzied whirling dance now,
wind peeling your last petals of adornment
unveiling a body of banal naked green.

It will be another year before you tempt, tease,
then torment our craving with seductive beauty.

Nelson Sartoris

For the Birds

finches, titmice, pine siskins, chickadees seek water
in juicy succulent leaves, but usually they wait on the seeds,
leaves meet their needs except in deep snow-covered freeze,
then on the seeds they will gladly feed.

perennial

autumn joy

sedum

in every season will provide and nurture avians

become

a gardener

seed them with sedum using a caring

green

thumb

LIFE CYCLE

from an icy mountain peak
late winter warmth releases
the first drops of liquid water

downward they drip
coalesce with others
trickle toward their target

enough now to flow
into a rapid rivulet
gravitating toward destiny

soon a stream forms
tumbling over rock and precipice
growing in size and roar

plummeting now over cascades
winding down and around hills
the mature river carves its way

it broadens on the plain
slows and meanders seeking
its saline mother

countless drops meld into the infinite sea . . .
then evaporation, precipitation, reincarnation
the river dies only to be reborn

Juggling Jaws

aerial gymnast
with acrobatic jaws
which preen feathers,
carry a tune
in flight,
grab a seed,
tumble it with ease,
crack shell,
discard hull,
consume kernel,
grab another seed,
repeat,
ferry the next back
to waiting gullets
of hatchlings
whose mouths
have yet to form
agile keratin jaws

Skyward

shining
gold
rock
rising
lucky
twinkling

it's written in them
hitch your wagon to them
shoot for them

but you'll likely miss
all too far away
reach instead

for what is monthly full
feel its pull
praise its phases
with poetic phrases
harvest its reflected glow
revel in its cast shadows
muse over its dark side
ebb and flow with its tides
sip its shine
howl in rhyme

Flight Envy

maestros of aerial motion
each species with signature mastery

thermal-seeking vultures **soar** in circles
cawing crows **flap** toward carrion
geese **knife** the airy vortex in a vee
majestic hawks **glide** through the wind
red baron swallows **helter-skelter** after insects
feisty chickadees **flit** acrobatically
goldfinches **undulate** in pulsated harmony
tonguing hummingbirds **hover** like helicopters
kingfishers **divebomb** for their dinner
tiny titmice **dart** to their target
pelicans **waft** over wave crests

earthbound penguins
lacking wing engines
fly only under water—
damning Darwin

WEEP FOR THE WILLOW

This majestic parasol by the road greeted me
as I drove by the last sixteen
of its hundred-year life.
its umbrel canopy touching the ground,
its early yellowing walls a sign spring was near.

Seventy years ago, one of its elder kin lived
in my grandparent's backyard, its green shroud
served as hideout, fort, playhouse, sanctuary.
Under veiled green protection a child's world
of play concealed from adult eyes.

Yesterday the regal roadside willow was gone,
another victim of the sharp blades
of mindless development,
something called progress
had decapitated it.

Weep for the willows of the world,
surely they weep for us.

Nelson Sartoris

I AND THOU

How unlike you I am,
rootless, while your roots
anchor in the land

Uncertain,
yet you are grounded firmly
between firmament and earth

Restless,
while you stand content
in a single space

Volatile,
but you are moored calm,
secure, proudly stoic

Frail,
as you stand fast,
strong against winds of change

Birds flee my presence,
they flock to safety
in your sheltering arms

I consume life's
essential element,
you provide it

I gravitate toward darkness,
you always reach
for the light

Yet when I pause, behold you,
honor you as tall sentry of life,
I am one with you

ERUPTION

On this bleak, cold,
windblown February day
I sense a slight tremor.

Outside my window I can almost
hear hyacinths break
through the frozen earth.

Almost immediately
my imagination savors the delicate scent
of anticipated blooms.

I don't need to look to confirm
this small green eruption,
I feel it, I know it's there.

I'll wait to savor blue,
purple, pink visual beauty
when blossoms usher spring.

Goose Talk

you hear them a mile away,
hear them honk, squawk, and yes, talk.
past dusk, almost totally dark, too dark
to see them, they've been grazing lush fields
far from their watery night home,

they tell those up front to *keep the pace,
stay in formation, cut drag and resistance,*
warn each other to *avoid one another,*
guide each other, *this way to the lake,*
its location somehow known to the leaders.

deafening now as they fly directly overhead
straight on course as the crow flies,
*keep together, another mile to go,
almost there, start to descend,
splashdown glidepath just ahead.*

their words, seemingly gibberish to us, speak clearly
to others in the skein, a language with no euphemisms,
no alternative meanings, no deceptions, no lies,
for there is no margin for error—
we should listen carefully.

Postcard

Having a terrible time

Place stamp here

No Vacancy

The world was bigger when I was born,
places were uninhabited, further away, difficult to visit,
pristine, authentic, untrampled by "civilized" man,
nature was natural, that was its lure, its downfall.

Cultures were genuine, unique,
not yet vulnerable to tourist mobs and their coins
that would transform and spoil them.

Southeast Asia was a land of enchanted gardens,
temples, pagodas, silk gowns, sampans,
dragons, kimono-clad concubines.
No longer.

Africa was dark, impenetrable, full of primitive tribes,
some peaceful, many not, wild animals everywhere,
ferocious beasts, migrating herds, unspoiled jungles.
No longer.

South America meant the Amazon jungle, piranha, primal people.
India a land of mystery, poverty, tigers, cobras.
Antarctica frozen, hostile, sterile, penguins, unapproachable.
Polynesia idyllic, virgin beaches, palm trees, hammocks.
No longer.

With quadrupled inhabitants and facile travel
our shrunken earth now interconnected subway stops.
Crowds congregate atop Everest,
throngs at cathedrals more carnival than spiritual,
beaches overflow with bodies and plastic debris,
more cruise ships than gondolas in Venice,
the Louvre so crowded Mona Lisa grimaces,
more tourists on animal safaris than wild creatures to see,
more beggars everywhere except in travel brochures,
McDonalds, Starbucks, T-shirts on every corner.

Too late to see anything different,
hordes of homogenized humanity all that's left.

The Fall

In that brief moment
everything changed—everything.
No more planning what to do tomorrow,
where to travel next month,
no more hosting dinner parties with friends,
no more open-ended, spur-of-the moments,
no more playful physical melding.
The agenda now proscribed—
pain, infirmity, hospital and doctor visits,
dutiful, debilitating caregiving.

The fall means their story must be altered,
the plot edited, the last few chapters abridged,
the ending no longer a mystery
to be unraveled sometime in the future,
the epilogue evident on today's page.

All that had been hoped for,
postponed, neglected, promised,
rectifications for moments squandered,
now fell into the realm of fallow fantasy.
The fall had become their winter.

LAST NIGHT

morning never rescued the night
light didn't surface
to quench the dark

the air never warmed
wind was stilled
water frozen

bird songs muted
animals inanimate
breath difficult

blackness in souls of some
smothered flames in others
all hope died

something was over
expectation of a new day betrayed
the Antichrist resurrected

God was gone
Abraham slayed Isaac
the plague continued

On a Scale of 1 to 10

Difficult to remember what a zero felt like,
either there was nothing to remember
or too long ago to recall.

Uncertain if I've ever experienced a ten,
a couple kidney stones might have qualified,
but how am I to know if something worse awaits

which might relegate kidney pain to a seven.
They say childbirth can be a ten, but as a male
I can't compare it to kidney stones or a broken arm.

If all that ails me is a one, two, or three,
it's not worth mentioning. If I do, I must be
a hypochondriac. Why waste the doctor's time?

What numbers distinguish pain that's throbbing
versus wrenching, excruciating versus burning,
sharp versus severe, deep versus dull?

And how am I to know if my level six pain
is similar to your six—or the doc's six?
This whole pain scale is a pain of ten in the ass.

MANHOOD IN AMERICA

American manhood role models:
    A former president
    Corrupt senators
    Greedy billionaires
    Brutal cops
    Deadbeat dads
    Televangelists
    Alcoholics and drug addicts
    Abusive husbands
    Macho gang members
    Hypocritical Christians
    Dishonest businessmen

Ritual passage to manhood in America:
    Get a pickup truck
    Buy some guns
    Get some ammo
    Put on some camo
    Bully someone
    Buy some beer
    Cover yourself with tattoos
    Help no one
    Hate people of color
    Dishonor women
    Never read a book

Easy to become an AmeriMan

THE HUNT

Americans live
in a shooting gallery
no license required
    to hunt down human quarry
    abundant game everywhere

PATRIOTISM

Not to a nation
Not to a land
Not to a flag
Not to a clan
Not any more

Mankind's callow
feral jingoisms
divide, estrange,
foment schisms
in a world grown small

On our overcrowded, overheated
sphere with shallow fanaticism,
My country right or wrong
has become a dangerous aphorism.
No longer can I pledge allegiance

to once hallowed borders and banners.
Tribal patriotism has become insanity
now and forever henceforth.
I'm loyal only to collective humanity
and our one common home called Earth.

Nelson Sartoris

MELTING POT

You forget—
when you arrived
we shared
food and bounty
from our pots with you.

Once sated, you
were rude guests,
defiled your hosts,
destroyed our food sources,
took our land.

You forget—
you lied when you
told us we could live
together in peace,
share earth's plenty.

You insisted we
conform to your ways,
melt into your pot,
said your America was a
melting pot for all peoples.

You forget—
your pot had room only
for northern Europeans,
not Africans, Asians,
indigenous people.

Now your stew congeals,
hardens, spoils, exposing
the poison of your selfish recipe,
rotting from greed,
hate, power.

Unsent Postcards

You forgot—
to honor your earth mother,
her trees, her animal children,
forgot to listen to the winds
of time, bend with them.

You are not the rulers
of the earth, but rather
passengers on her journey.
You would have been wise
to have melted into our pot.

Kids in the Backseat

No matter how long—or short—
the family road trip
the final ten percent
was always torture.

If three hundred miles,
kids were sure to act up
those last thirty; a final half hour
of tantrums, turf wars, tempers, tears.

Somehow they knew when the ten percent
barrier was breached, homestretch begun,
when otherwise effective placations
abruptly lost their allure.

"I see something in the car that begins with W"
now prompted just more whining.
License plate hunts only turned up
new states of chaos.

The Hangman word game
brought me to rope's end
as they transformed the backseat
into a Hang 'em High movie set.

Modern mandatory seatbelts limited
"stay on your side" battles and videos
served well the first ninety percent,
yet regardless the distance, at the end
of the journey you always arrived in Hell.

Dissonance

The swarm
has grown larger,
the relentless buzz intensifies

Bells which once chimed softly
from a distant church tower
now clang incessantly

Snake pit has filled,
their collective hiss amplifies
to a piercing shrill

The din drowns patter of rain,
whistle of wind through trees
a waning memory

Whisper of ripples coming ashore
now inaudible, deadened
by deafening waves crashing

The combined clamor presently pulses
and whooshes in rhythmic sync
with my heartbeat

Voices and music swamped
as they sink into the cacophonic muck
of pulsatile tinnitus

Gaps

of course she was no longer the same
as when they wed, neither was he,
their skin and muscle tone withered,

postures slumped, energy diminished,
lines and wrinkles, hair grayed, not as soft—
all gradual metamorphoses,

slow changes barely discerned
through a lifetime together,
mutual aging melding life's stages.

then one day he couldn't help but acknowledge
distinct hesitations in her speech,
first when searching for names

of persons or flowers or places.
he willingly filled in the gaps even as
they occurred more frequently.

she struggled to recall yesterday's conversations,
calendar appointments, restaurants where they'd dined,
places they'd traveled became vague mysteries.

she began to misplace and lose things,
every day more time spent looking for papers,
utensils, accessories she had earlier in the day.

when speaking to her he'd have to repeat himself,
as if his words, however soft or direct,
must first penetrate an armored aura to register.

he hoped she was just not paying attention
or was distracted, then realized attention
was another cognition being lost.

he found himself exhausted thinking for two,
found himself alone in her presence, found himself
ever fearful someday she'd forget who he was.

ENNUI

housed and fed,
not working or parenting,
many while away the hours,
days, months, years

with solitaire, crosswords,
video games, Facebook, TV series,
searching for something
to occupy time until death,

anything to escape the boredom
of existence, to avoid one's self.
a few lucky ones lose awareness
in creative or helpful endeavors

but most fear an afterlife where
eternal boredom awaits.

WHITE PICKET FENCES

Expectation of a lifetime partner
culturally imprinted, with passion now
in his heart, stirring in his groin,

she becomes the vision personified,
the promise of intimacy,
end of loneliness.

But once inside the picket fence
cold reality unfolds, paint peels,
her vowed fervor faded, false.

Interior fences, defenses erected,
Maginot lines with no exits,
Sartre's bungalow of Hell.

So easy to enter,
so hard to escape,
this contractual rite often

a license to neglect love,
an unholy legal cement
binding antipathy.

Only meaningful glue:
abiding investment in each other
and daily mutual affection.

If absent, easy disentanglement,
no lawyers with their sharp
expensive knives.

FRENZY

tempest of our time
    swirls
                surges ever faster
blowing away
    all that seemed stable
leaving us breathless
            trying to preserve normalcy

    but the fury quickens
a fierce banshee
          unsure of its own destiny
feverishly accelerates
    pushes us
             relentlessly
        leaving everything familiar in the debris
    of obsolete yesterdays

where are we going
why the hurry
    we struggle for air as we try to stay
            in a race
                to the edge of a cliff
to see who gets there first

if we could only
    dampen the pulse
        ease the pace
           slow the howling
              whirlwind of change
                  we might have a chance

to breathe

INFERNAL COMBUSTION

Rev that engine, pedal to the floor
power the roar that says you're hardcore
bad to the bone, Mr. Testosterone

Peel out, squeal those tires
lay down tread, full speed ahead
roll coal, toss aloft black exhaust

Show them you're a badass
a real rebel, no matter
the cash for rubber and gas

Blast rap in decibels from Hell
blurred words, low-class and crass
harass the masses as you exit pell-mell

>
> Sipping coffee
> at an outdoor café
> the annoyed woman
> he sought to impress
> mutters to herself
> *Hey, macho man, if you're so cool, so smart,*
> *why don't you blare out Brahms or Mozart?*

Postcard

Place stamp here

The food is fantastic

Garnish

My Manhattan—
　　Three cubes of ice,
　　Three parts Woodford Reserve Bourbon,
　　One part Noilly Prat Sweet Vermouth,
　　Dash of Fee Brothers Aztec Chocolate Bitters

Delicious, yet still incomplete,
no bonus, no bonanza,
no bounty, no booty,
it's pie alamode without ice cream.

It begs for an Italian Amarena wild tart black cherry
　　to marinate in the alcohol,
　　add a hint of fruit flavor,
　　eyeball for anticipated pleasure,
　　savor at drink's end.

It's the prize in the box of Cracker Jack,
　　just caramel corn and peanuts without it
It's the pearl in the oyster,
　　just a beach souvenir without it
It's the Babe Ruth card in a Topps bubble gum pack,
　　just chalky stale gum without it
It's the secret decoder ring in the Kix cereal box,
　　just puffed-cornmeal without it

It's the cherry that fills life's bowl.

TASTES EXTRAORDINAIRE

Outdoor café off the beaten tourist path, lovely blue-green eyes dance across the table at me, a perfect late light lunch to lustfully share.

First, a bottle of Chilean Concha y Toro Terrunyo Carmenere, deep red/violet, a robust nose, the essence of blueberries with toasty hints of spices and cassis enlivens our eager palates.

A plate of Jersey blue cheese from Switzerland, veined with grey, blue, and white molds, its buttery, juicy, assertive blueing flavor arouses our ardent appetites.

Along with the cheese, rich flaky Browne's scotch-whisky-cured smoked salmon from coastal Oregon, creamy and silky, its smoky scotch sensual sweetness tantalizes our tongues.

Finally, to accompany the last precious pours of the Carmenere, exotic Amedei Tuscany Porcelana dark chocolate, its delicate spice laden cooling sensation sonorously massages our mouths.

This culinary combination is romantic oral bliss, yet our hunger is not sated, I look into her eyes and whisper, Taste buds aren't the only sense responsible for this ecstasy. The nose, eyes, even touch are involved.

What if, I ask, *the Carmenere tasted like Jersey blue cheese? and the blue cheese tasted like the Carmenere? What if the Porcelana chocolate smelled like Browne's smoked salmon?*

Or the smoked salmon tasted like dark chocolate? What if the wine smelled like the whisky smoked salmon and the chocolate looked and felt like moldy blue cheese?

They'd all be the same great tastes, but we would spit everything out, I said sagaciously, *because most of taste is in the expectation—part is visual, part is anticipated texture, part is presumed aroma.*

These sterling insights were hard to digest for this now odious blue-green eyed filly. She wouldn't dine with me again. I guess she didn't have the stomach for great savoir faire. Something didn't suit her taste.

Raw Truth

I would never waste a nickel
on a hated jar of pickles.
I'd puke more than spittle,
if I ate just a little,
worse still, some have added dill,
dreadful swill that makes me ill.

I'm not being comical, it'll
land me in the hospital.
Tell me why anyone hungers
to alter yummy cucumbers,
they've no need of vinegar and brine,
enjoy them raw, they're already fine,

And there's no merit in cooking carrots,
they come with crunch that's 24-karat,
why bother to devour boiled cauliflower,
it tastes great without a roiling hot shower,
cooking won't enhance broccoli's flavor,
eat snap peas raw and get more to savor.

We would catch hell-if-we ever cook celery,
we'd miss the loud munch of a fresh bunch at lunch,
even crispy cabbage is better ravaged
without unnecessary boiling damage,
and don't put onions or their cousins in ovens,
they're far more indulgent eaten raw and pungent.

There's nothing more outlandish
than a dish of boiled radish,
and don't cook asparagus into a mush,
chomping fresh tips is much more nutritious
before we finish, don't spoil spinach in a hot pan,
it's better eaten raw than from Popeye's can.

And much to their credit, no one cooks lettuce,
time to get over this cooked veggie fetish.

That First Delicious Apple

not much knowledge
in only one bite

the good resides
at the core
of knowing

evil lies
in not gorging
on the whole tree

so devour bushels
of enlightening
slices

until you finally know
how little you
know

and are humbled
by that knowledge

Menu Guide

Use your cervelle to figure out that
      headcheese isn't dairy and hamburgers
      don't come from pigs.

Good news for vegans; you can order Welsh rabbit,
      animal crackers, or mincemeat pie.
      Just don't say the words too loudly.

Since you don't cook cookies,
      shouldn't we call them bakies.

Sweetbreads are gluten free.

Truffles are a trifle troubling,
      could be fungi,
      could be chocolate.

There's no fowl play if you order Bombay Duck.

We live in a digital world, so enjoy the lady fingers.

Bear claws won't harm you
      if they are made from scratch.

It's nuts that Rocky Mountain oysters
      don't come from the sea - best not to order them
      with a side of lamb fries.

And for those just a little bit racist,
      chocolate Devil's food or white Angel food cake.

Rafter Disaster

there's little laughter
in the only rafter I've known,
I should be in the wild
with my undomesticated kind,
instead, I'm caged with fellow inmates
awaiting the hereafter.

soon I'll lie supine, insulted,
akimbo deconstructed,
a warm, tan-encrusted,
lusted-after centerpiece
ready to be sculpted—
while you give thanks.

Day Break

despondent
decrepit
desolate
hungry
need coffee
need breakfast

How would you like your eggs?

    too late in life for sunny-side up
    my brain's already fried
    thoughts scrambled
    heart hard-boiled
    soul deviled

Like life, I'd prefer mine over . . . easy

Nelson Sartoris

QUEST

I wander the streets of life
just to be going somewhere,
retracing steps that have
already led nowhere.

I pass the moments of life
seeking reasons to go forward,
bored with everything I do
to keep from being bored.

I sit probing meaning in life
wondering who I am, what I know,
where I come from,
when I most go.

I stand near the end of life
pondering why I've been here,
why this planet, why at this time,
why this fear, when I'll disappear.

I lay my soul bare, confront my demons
face-to-face once more, suffer their attack,
know they'll defeat me again. Been to Hell
before, know there's no easy way back.

Many things can kill a man,
there are many ways to die,
many so far have had their chance,
some still left to try.

So empty, so alone,
how long can I survive
being wholly broken,
living barely alive.

Nelson Sartoris

UPSIDE DOWN

Heaven's above? up?
somewhere out there in the solar system?
the milky way?
the galaxy?
the empty ether between galaxies?

No, up is Dante's ninth circle of Hell
frigid, unbreathable, sterile,
infinite nothingness

Heaven is down
here on this blue marble
with green trees,
oxygen, blue waters,
flowers, soil, rain,
real birds (not mythical
cherubs or angels), music,
art, poetry, sunsets,

and dogs, for heaven's sake

Drawing Horses

Artists who know say horses
are hard to draw,
often I tried when young.

I longed to capture them, conquer
them on paper, their whole bodies
from hoof to haunches to mane.

Never could get proportions true,
couldn't delineate muscle and sinew,
distorted clown horses always the result.

I finally succeeded drawing their heads,
but only profiles, something about
both eyes face-to-face unnerved me,

spirit, power, majesty
of horses perhaps too fugitive
to capture on canvas . . . humbling.

Yet—
I can draw horses
better than they can draw me.

Take that, proud steed!
I use your hairs for my brushes,
your hooves can't even hold a brush.

AT THE END OF THE DAY

I flinch, fragile nerves fray
when I hear the cliché,
"at the end of the day."

I'm always tempted to recite
with mocking spite and snide delight,
"at the end of the day . . . is night."

There are definitely other ways
to convey what one's trying to say
without using that dreadful cliché:

> *To make a long story short*
> *Taking everything into account*
> *Not to beat around the bush*
>
> *To sum it all up*
> *All things considered*
> *For all intents and purposes*
>
> *In a nutshell*
> *To put it concisely*
> *When push comes to shove*
>
> *When you get right down to it*
> *When all is said and done*
> *This is the bottom line*

But at the end of the day
there's no other way to say,
"at the end of the day"
except with another cliché.

CARNIVAL OF LIFE

Step right up
Punch your ticket
Ride the earth

You've been waiting
in line for generations
Now it's your turn

Strap yourself in
Hold on tight
for the time of your life

It's a short ride
but it'll scare
the shit out of you

Your stomach
will be in your throat
as the ride nears the end

Time to cut the cord
Let out a yell
Life's roller coaster begins

Savor this blood-curdling
short ride to Hell
It will be over soon—

for all of us

Close Quarters

Escape from each other had held them together,
work, friends, dining, shopping not shared,
both busy with individual agendas.

Home contacts civil but brief, conversations
more like reports, home meals seldom as a couple,
mattress usually cold between the warm spots.

From outside, appearance of togetherness,
within their walls personal spaces void of intimacy,
more partnership than pairing.

Then COVID lurks outside forcing them inside,
now both work from home, closeness inescapable,
outside attractions, distractions now nullified.

Their only hope, or hell, now resides in one another,
slowly, quietly, they pause, listen to each other,
slowly, quietly, they rediscover each other.

Candles come out for mutually prepared dinners,
conversations become spiced with humor, eye contact,
the cold mattress space slowly warms.

With vaccines imminent each anxiously awaits
the time their separate worlds reopen,
each ponders what immunity will bring.

Day Lily

This very moment
I will forget the past
Begin anew, clean slate
Leave all the pain behind
No regrets of yesterdays

This very moment
I will stop planning the future
I will have no fear of tomorrows
No agenda will destroy the present
No expectations will cloud happenstance

This very moment
I will forget time
Seek harmony with the now
Make the most of every breath
Savor today's sun as does the day lily

This very moment...
I am such a fool.
I deceive myself again,
for I am but the archive of my yesterdays,
the hunger for my tomorrows

WATERING HOLE

A graveyard of broken lives,
a beer-lubricated confessional
full of macho souls gone sour,
a temporary comfort-station
in a world turned cold, a world
that will never warm, a world
where personal songs resonate
with the blues.

This is where you end up when love
falls out of your life. You hang with,
get advice from others who have
also lost love; the blind lead the blind.
You long for that elusive woman
who will nestle in your arms, smile,
talk softly, look at, not through, you.
If you had her, you wouldn't be here.

You brag about great moments
in your life, most of it barely true banter,
tell bawdy tales everyone has already heard.
With strained laughter you drink
another beer to avoid crying in it.
Then slowly, one-by-one, return to a place
called home where loneliness accelerates.
You'll be back tomorrow.

HUMAN ENIGMA

Such beauty, such ugliness
Such potential, such waste
Such intellect, such ignorance
Such affection, such hatred
Such creativity, such destruction

Inventive enough to make guns,
    evil enough to use them.
Informed enough to write books,
    ignorant enough not to read them.
Industrious enough to amass fortunes,
    greedy enough to hoard them.
Ingenious enough to create television,
    crass enough to fill it with inanity.
Inspired enough to produce life-saving drugs,
    callous enough to price them out of reach.
Innovative enough to make smart phones,
    stupid enough to fill them with spam and robocalls.

Introspective enough to savor spirituality,
    blind enough to fill it with dogma.

No U-Turn

took a wrong turn
early in life,
got lost,
spent the rest of it trying
to get back
to the former me.

now at four score
finally realize trying
to go back
holds you back
prevents you from creating
another you.

being lost just means
you are somewhere new.
no turning back, there's life ahead.

UNLIKE TODAY

I'm dying—yet I've barely lived.
Born into a culture of behavioral norms
geared to controlling uncertainty,
I fulfilled society's expectations.

College, career, marriage, children,
planned for a predictable future,
worked to eradicate chance, diminished serendipity,
controlled my environment, created unsurprising
tomorrows.

Welcome, my son, welcome to the machine.

Better to have lived more capriciously—
flexible, fluid, adaptive,
malleable, spontaneous,
unbound by the customs of culture,

and live every tomorrow unlike today.

INTERRUPTIONS

Walking is falling interrupted

Standing is walking interrupted

Sitting is standing interrupted

Reclining is sitting interrupted

Death is reclining interrupted

INTERNAL DIALOGUE

the conversation drones on,
cogent arguments on both sides,
but neither hears the other,
just two voices colliding,
volume escalates,
each bored with
the other's diatribe,
how to persuade the other
when the other is a simpleton,
clarity of thought lost
in the dissonance,
resolution, as usual,
impossible.

talking to oneself
is a fool's mission,
since only a fool
would listen.

Evolving Invocation

Our Darwin
who started a revolution,
profane some call thy name
but from old species we come, into new we go,
on earth, creatures spawned through evolution.

Give us this day, our DNA, and time for mutation
and forgive them their stupidity
who believe with rigidity
that Earth be just 6,000 years old.

Lead us not into temptation of the faux ism of creation
for science is the wisdom and the power and the story—
of enlightened civilization.

BONDING

The name is Bond ... James Bond,

    he of fast cars and sexy blonds
    both of which he was very fond.

    many pretenders —Brosnan, Moore, Craig,
    others unnoteworthy, only one true Bond --

The name is Connery ... Sean Connery,

    the ornery, contrary, 007 drollery spy who broke
    every boundary of roguery and escaped from every
    life-threatening quandary with suave refinery.

    no love doctor from Russia ever put
    more gold on the fingers or diamonds
    on forever beautiful bodies of sirens.

    never say never again, but you'd
    have to live more than twice to find
    another Bond with enough thunderballs
    to score with one of the world's
    classiest, top-drawer whores—

The name is Galore ... Pussy Galore.

ODE TO THE DOUBLE HELIX

```
          nucleic                          repeat
   acids                              repeat
      coil                                 evolve
         base                                 allele
            pairs                                         novel
               code                             mutate
         copy                                repeat
   link                                 repeat
      uncoil                               repeat
         new                                     repeat
            life                                             repeat
         repeat                              life
      repeat                              new
   repeat                           uncoil
      repeat                            link
         repeat                             copy
            mutate                                     code
         novel                              pairs
      allele                           base
   evolve                           coil
      repeat                            acids
         repeat                             nucleic
```

without this chemically induced twist
the universe is just physics, no biology
if no double helix, only elements, rocks, energy

coils, the core of all life
essential for progeny, for growth, for thought, for will
responsible for Darwin's finches, tiger stripes, giant Sequoias,
butterflies, dandelions erupting through concrete

its drive toward replication and mutation insatiable
this coiled life force compels its hosts to eat, to eat other life
life needs life to live, it chews with double helix teeth

It's Official

Nike, the official shoe of MLB
Wilson, the official football of the NFL
KIA, the official car of the NBA
Coke, the official drink of NASCAR

Time for nonprofits and charities to get in on the action—
the official hammer of Habitat for Humanity
the official condom of Planned Parenthood
the official hearing aid of AARP
the official bucket of the Salvation Army
the official mayonnaise of the Mayo Clinic
the official tire of Rotary International
the official clothes hanger of Goodwill
the official non-alcoholic beer of AA
the official wallet of Samaritan's Purse
the official bandage of the American Red Cross
the official song of the YMCA

A Past Future

Old future gone...
evaporated
before I got there

Wasted...
too many yesterdays
waiting for its arrival, now
I can't get there from here

Paralyzed...
by the past
difficult to construct
a new future

Only tools available...
the debris
of broken dreams
and past failure

AT THE MARKET

I first noticed her
when we both reached for the same bunch of bananas.
We smiled as I deferred and chose a different bunch.
Something about her smile indicated she hadn't worn it
recently, so was a bit surprised, yet pleased by it.

I encountered her next when I entered the salad dressing aisle,
our carts almost colliding. Again, we smiled, easier this time.
She was about my age, trim, pensive, a quiet peace about her.
Later, our paths met again at the ice cream freezer,
this time our smiles turned into audible chuckles.

As usual, only one checkout lane open. Waiting in line,
she rolled her cart up behind mine. I wanted to ask,
What's your name? Do you shop here often? Can I buy you coffee?
But all I said was, *You have a lot fewer items than I do, so please
go ahead of me.* She thanked me and did, then that smile again.

As she put her bagged items in her cart and I unloaded mine
onto the counter the clerk asked me if I'd found everything
I was looking for. Calmly, sincerely I answered, *I was looking
for serenity, companionship, and world peace. Were you hiding them?*
The woman ahead looked back, laughed aloud, *They're all sold out.*

Dust

Born in a star, my body elements
soon to return to dust.

Would that I could chart the journey
my current atoms took to become me.
For what creatures, what plants,
was my dust once essential?

Where will my dust travel
when it takes leave of me?
Into what new creatures will it give life?
Where in the universe will I be dispersed?

What of the atoms of these printed words . . .
will they be recycled one day through the pen
of a future poet who will arranged
them more skillfully?

And how is it possible my current atoms
can create memories, which have no matter,
no dust? How can elements without memory
make memory? Then lose it all in dust.

Dimmer

      body exhausted,
      burdened with pain of years,
      sleep beckons as refuge,
      yet the mind still races,
      chased by worry, memory,
      tomorrow

no on/off switch
            only a dimmer
      which paralyzes me
      in mental fog limbo,
      strands me in arcane moments
      between consciousness
      and sought oblivion

———

      in the silent darkness
      of early morning,
      over-rated sentience stirs,
      is this still part of a dream
      or the end of one?
      consciousness be damned

no off/on switch
            only a dimmer,
      which slowly erases
      dreamy mindlessness
      and terrifyingly reveals
      the mad world
      I will inhabit today

Nelson Sartoris

Postcard

Place stamp here

Never coming back here

AMERICAN RELAPSE

We thought you were dying,
slowly, yes, but dying nonetheless.
Many reveled in your anticipated demise
as they would the eradication of a deadly virus.
It was as if a vaccine to combat evil
had arrived and inoculated enough people
to create herd immunity.

Your pending death gave hope everywhere,
in all arenas new colors blossomed,
new leaders of the other emerged
to assume positions of power, respect,
admiration. Civility seemed to reign.

We were wrong. You lay dormant feigning death,
hibernating in restrained politeness,
faking tolerance, masquerading color-blindness,
just waiting for the infection to rekindle,
for the wound to reopen, for medicinal cocktails
of hate and fear to release you, give you license,
encourage you, praise you.

Armed now with new weapons and loathing,
your diseased face erupts, surfaces anew.
Your malignancy spreads consuming
the soul of the country again,
as it has for four hundred years.

DOTAGE

easy getting into
bed, hopeless falling restfully asleep
    hundreds of books on my
        shelves, dwindling memory of what they hold
            bathroom cabinet full of
                medicines, body and mind empty of wellness
                    comfortable sleek new
                        car, few places I still long to go
                            workshop packed with
                                tools, nothing else I wish to build
                                accounts flush with
                                    wealth, little I desire to purchase
                                    many clocks on my
                                    walls, little time left

END TIMES

In spartan dim rooms they sit or lie,
marking time until there is none,
occasional cognitive moments vacillate
between foggy memories and regret.

Most time is spent in a semi-conscious haze
or nibbling at unappetizing food
they barely recognize or taste,
and cannot remember eating moments after.

A few curio keepsakes surround them,
precious, though they can't remember why,
last remains from decades of accumulation,
last links with a once vibrant life.

A small TV blares daytime programming,
inanity to which they pay little attention,
yet the flickering screen is their only connection
to an outside world that would just as soon forget them.

Occasional visitors interrupt the reverie of malaise,
awkward moments for those who feel obligated to visit,
but then cannot wait to leave, awkward too for many
of the visited who cannot wait for them to do so.

Mostly women, suffering the price of longevity,
bearing the burden, as always, of duty, this time
to the sanctity of life, even what little remains.
Still, they fade into another long sleepless night
hoping they will not see the dawn.

Pronouns

Introduced to someone recently
who was probably a woman,
but in these politically correct times
I hesitate to label anyone prematurely.

The name given: Jane.
my first impression apparently correct,
was assured when Jane offered pronouns:
She/her/hers.

She asked mine. Took me a while to answer
since I'm not interested in anyone's pronouns,
more concerned with their adjectives.
So I told her mine:

Caring, honest, amicable. She said,
You're rude, insensitive and a smart ass.
I figured out what her adjectives were
without having to ask.

FINAL RENAISSANCE

we pretended it would last forever
some even believed it
most incapable of imagining otherwise

buildings would get bigger, airplanes faster,
technology better, space travel easier,
medicines would cure everything

but our planet was too small, too depleted,
too warm, too poisoned, too tired,
and we and the viruses kept multiplying

barriers and collisions became inevitable
resources exhausted, breaking points reached,
civilized culture collapsed

it had happened before, Egyptians,
Romans, Mayans, Anasazi crashed,
dispersed into the remains of nature

only to rise again in a different form,
a different place, in a different time,
each new culture thinking itself immortal

but this time it is global
nowhere new to go, nothing left
to fuel engines of civilization rebirth

there are too many of us, too blind, too cock-sure,
too few of us wise enough to seek harmony instead of
ephemeral power, endless wrath, another dollar

NEARER

I guess it has always been this way.
I'd just been too young to recognize it,
too busy, too preoccupied with life, with plans
for the future, just couldn't be bothered.

Finitude was but a distant mirage,
something I could postpone 'til later,
not certain when later awakened my brain
but once that awareness took residence

it never leaves . . . never.
You cannot unknow it—
Life becomes a near-death experience
which gets nearer every day.

NEVER AGAIN

White European invaders,
Native American genocide,
Eighteen million erased.
    We say, "Never again!"

Turk butchers,
Armenian/Assyrian genocide
One million erased.
    We assert, "Never again!"

Nazi exterminators,
Jewish genocide,
Six million erased.
    We vow, "Never again!"

Khmer Rouge executioners,
Cambodian peasant genocide,
Two million erased.
    We declare, "Never again!"

Communist Chinese eradicators,
Muslim Uyghur genocide,
Millions being erased.
    We exclaim, "Not again!
    We said never again!"

But it's never
    "Never again."
        It's always...
            "When."

Unmasked

finally, masks come off,
meeting face-to-face
for the first time
assessments begin.
are you still you?
am I still me?
concealed tragedy
awaits under comedic masks

we have all aged—
aged more than
chronological time.
smiles weakened,
brows chiseled,
dimness in our eyes,
lilt in our steps lost.

stress, angst, sadness
carved years from us,
time elapsed
hope collapsed
joy evaporated
sock eclipsed by buskin.

MORE TO LOSE

Freedom isn't just another word
for nothing left to lose,
it's now a rationale we misuse
for selfish behaviors that abuse
civilized views we refuse

Freedom's become the ruse
used to excuse
times we choose
not to be responsible
    to pass gun legislation
    to get a vaccination
    to heed climate alteration
    to mask germ propagation

Freedom's become the rallying cry
used to justify
conduct that vilifies
prudent rules
on which civil society relies

It's as if escaping King George's tyranny
was license to propagate defiant errancy
in whatever the hell we may wish
no matter how foolish or mulish

Freedom's become irresponsibility
cloaked in jingoistic nationality,
it's not a patriotic opus,
rather a moronic onus
leading us to barbarous immorality

Beating the drum
for unbridled freedom
will not lead us to Eden
instead we'll succumb
to ruinous free-dumb

PO
ET
RY Journal, February 2021

the entire issue,
poems by those incarcerated.

each triggers my innermost fear,
imagined wounds of confinement bleed,
stir-crazed madness looms every minute,

could I find solace writing poetry?
about nature? beauty? love?
what stimulus could kindle my pen?

as cell door clangs closed muses muted,
words barred, verse shackled
when neither tree nor sky visible.

body penned in a barren cage,
poems locked in my head,
the only theme that might escape—

f r e e d o m

WIDOWER

Though our back yards adjoined, the old man
rarely spoke. Through all those years he never
yelled at my kids to keep off his grass,
keep their balls and toys off his property,
never scolded them for being too loud.

But what was he thinking? Did the noise
anger him? Was he irritated by the fun
and boisterous vitality? Did he go inside
cursing the disregard of his property line?
Who knew? Never asked him, never probed.

He lived in that yet unknown lonely world of old.
Now, decades later, I live in that same realm,
and as my young next-door neighbor
frolics with his loud and spirited kids, I finally
understand what the old man felt—envy.

STIGMATA

The most visible ones
vertical, handspan in length,
one on each knee, like train-tracks,
insertion portals for metal.

Apparent next to one rail, a two inch
long wide, glossy, aged scab from
a childhood scooter encounter
with a metal wire fence.

Harder to see, two lower-back
surgical reminders of disc repairs,
from which continuing trauma
belies the minor cicatrices.

Close inspection reveals many
small hand battle casualties
from tools, knives, struggle,
anger, carelessness.

Impossible to see, unless scrutinized
by eyes able to peer into my soul,
huge scars of ersatz love carved
crisscross on my heart.

DECEPTION

Were his poems about an imaginary love,
just fantasies and reveries of desire, a siren goddess
he created with words to satisfy a deep need for
intimacy, a phantom birthed by a hopeless romantic?

Or—did his poems expose a loving paramour
to whom these odes were directed, did they
endear him to her susceptible heart, did they
curry favors of heightened passion?

If so, why did he share them with others, why not
keep them private, hidden from judgmental eyes,
did he intentionally make them public as a ruse
to protect the secret by exposing it?

No one would believe him that reckless, that
enthralled with danger, that by teasing the truth
he was gambling it helped conceal the ardor, that
hinting a potential secret love would help hide it.

Or—were they written to fabricate a coquettish
Lorelei his cold life-partner would think real,
tormenting her with a seductive possibility
of all that she wasn't and wouldn't give?

SURROGATES

Young men
different flags
different languages
different customs
different beliefs
bear no grudge
against each other

Old men
full of hubris
power
dreams of glory
hate
bear grudges
against other old men

Young men
learn from old men
how and who
to hate

Old men
send young men
to fight young men
sent by other old men

Young men
die

Old men
live on

Memory Shackles

some
memories   are
like mountain   peaks
eternal, unscalable,   impossible to
traverse, so forbidding   I spend my days
longing for night so they might disappear in sleep,
only to find slumber thwarted by them. I spend restless nights
longing for dawn, hoping light might reveal a path around them.

Ninth Decade

death has awakened inside of me
    its seeds planted at conception
gravity, now grown stronger,
    commands my constant attention
balance now a tightrope walk
    over ground increasingly hardened
strength ebbs as joint cement solidifies
    hand tremors amplify steadily
naps call more frequently
    precursors for the long sleep

Postcard

Place stamp here

Greetings from yesterday

Nelson Sartoris

Mature Meanings

word meanings mature.
when young, "terminal" referred
to transportation—
    airports and railway stations.
    now it's the end of the line.

YESTERDAY'S SUNDAYS

Sundays were Sunday then,
perhaps because most stores were closed,
fast-food lures didn't exist,
maybe because there were no robocalls,
no internet to interrupt competitive
Monopoly and Parcheesi games
or rapt focus on *Chicago Tribune* features and comics.
The only phone calls, short, pricey
long-distance hellos to faraway family.

No one-hundred-plus TV channels twenty-four
hours a day—only the Indian test pattern
until 5pm when Mary Hartline's Super Circus
appeared on that prized new tiny
black and white screen after multiple fiddlings
with tin-foiled rabbit ears.

We were home. It was Sunday.
It was quiet, save for the customary
early afternoon family dinner gathering,
chicken and rice and peas and pie,
comfort food—long before it needed a name.
As the day wore on our ears were tuned
to big band crooners or Cubs' games
on the big mahogany Philco, more furniture than radio,
then a family walk to and through Jackson Park
to meet neighbors on similar missions.

Hushed book immersion occupied
the precious waning hour before bedtime
and the coming dreaded, dutiful awakening
to Monday realities—work day, school day, wash day.
Tranquility would come again in a week.

WAY OF THE WORLD

We drove all the way to the beach
All the way there we listened to the Top 40
Her new bathing suit had come all the way from New York
We swam all the way out past the sandbar
The burgers we ate weren't cooked all the way through
Drank cheap wine that burned all the way down our throats
Wrapped towels all the way around us in the sand
I carried her all the way back to the car
She leaned all the way back on the seat
I put my arms all the way around her wet body
It was hard to get her wet bathing suit all the way off
She breathed deeply all the way through heavy foreplay
But it was 1958 so we didn't go all the way

A Dollar. A Day.

California shore, perfect day,
sun ablaze, welcoming waves,
just his wife and kids and a lone beachcomber
whose gaze is fixed on sand treasures,
modest breakers ebb back into seabed froth
only to roll ashore once more.

Their young kids frolic in ceaseless surf,
last light fades well after rays of Ra
have sunk into Neptune's Pacific realm.
Summoning his kids to finally take leave
for that sleepy ride back to the hotel
a glimmering beach gem grabs his eye.

A sand dollar, whole and intact,
a delicate porcelain wonder.
Cradling it, he tucks it in a car trunk recess,
perhaps with hope it will forever serve
as memento of this glorious day—
now forty years ago.

Relegated to a box when they returned to Ohio,
its skeleton languished in that cardboard coffin
until rediscovered during this death cleaning,
his wife's sands of time having now ebbed from his shore.
It crumbles the moment he picks it up—
a reminder of what life's worth when it's gone.

Unsent Postcards

BENCHMARKS

Fancy autos of the '60s sprouted huge fins,
as if to suggest they could simply fly or swim.

Station wagons became a '70s staple,
suburban homes had at least one in their stable.

Minivans arrived on the scene in the '80s,
instantly a big hit with parenting ladies.

In the 90s all attention turned to the wheels,
low profile tires, jumbo rims, spinners, all big deals.

The new century spawned the age of SUVs,
rapidly they've ballooned into monstrous Humvees.

And now the spotlight is on LED taillights
and sleek sculpted side panels like rockets in flight.

All this design glitz was nothing but a ploy
to divert our focus as they ruined our joy.

They substituted buckets, took away our bench seats,
put in center consoles so our thighs couldn't meet.

Damn things prevented us from getting too chummy,
no more could you drive with your arm 'round your honey,

Gone now was the need for necker-knobs on the wheel,
when with one hand you steered so the other could feel.

I'd rather be driving my old '53 Merc
with its palatial bench seat its number one perk.

ANCIENT PATHS

New paths, new roads,
new continents, new planets
ever faster, through air,
through space.

Yet the baggage we carry
can never be shed,
it's the same burden ancients
bore on primitive paths,

struggles of evil and good,
selfishness or selflessness,
love and hate, power or service,
the millstone luggage of torn souls.

And always—awareness and fear
of the post-finitude mystery.
Modern paths lead where ancient
paths led—the void of unbeing.

Indelible Ink

The first ones I recall
were deltoid one-liners:

Mom   **Judy**   *USS Hornet*

simple sailor and soldier badges,
usually hidden, not considered tasteful.

I also remember numbers
forever etched on inside forearms
of survivors.

Rarely seen again until century twenty-one
when derma ink flowed profusely into skin,
hyped in part by athletes, rock and rap stars.

An explosion of ankle butterflies,
tramp stamps, bracelets, flowers, dragons,
then neck and face billboards signaling,
"I don't want a real job."

Entire bodies now canvas for
indelible art to set wearers apart
from society's mainstream.

Decoration or desecration?

Dark Spot

Look, Jane, see Spot run.
Run, Spot, run.

For decades we learned
to read through Dick and Jane.
We learned about Spot, Puff,
and baby sister, Sally. We learned
that father worked and mother
cooked and did laundry, that Americans
lived in nice houses with pretty lawns
in safe neighborhoods.

We learned something else.
There were no dark faces
in Dick and Jane's neighborhood,
they were invisible,
hidden, didn't count,
learned Dick and Jane were entitled.

Children learned how to read
and believe these lies.

PUTTING IT TO REST

for seventy years it's been on Smoky Park highway
a now blighted commercial city route
the interstate bypassed long ago

once a welcome sight for post-war vacationers
the ten-room Rest Haven motel now a rundown
rendezvous for cheap short afternoon trysts

busted screen doors, rusty window air conditioners
crumbling shingles, paint-starved rotted clapboard siding
weeds in the cracks of a long-empty swimming pool

crooked neon sign always blinking "vacancy"
blacktop parking lot full of potholes, empty but
for two battered pickups and an old station wagon

inside unseen, but certainly unseemly—musty odor,
rust-stain bathroom sinks, peeling wallpaper
thin worn bedspreads with many stories to tell

grapevine says property just sold, demolition soon,
the few guests who'll notice will find a bed elsewhere,
rumor is a Dollar store is coming

Nelson Sartoris

REGRETTABLE

too many todays
dwelling on yesterdays
days spent not in the world
but in recesses of memory
some echoes pleasant, more sad
both a waste of today's time

remembrance burdened with
could, would, should,
deep rabbit holes
where loss and moments
of numbing regret
are never forgotten

too many todays
planning for tomorrows
establishing expectations
inevitably not met
days defined by agenda
a self-annulling mindset

agendas offer security
from chaos and uncertainty
but at the price
of spontaneous opportunity
and serendipitous
possibility

better to have ignored
yesterdays and tomorrows,
time spent on either
meant todays' time borrowed
loans not repayable
with remorse nor sorrow

Rural Sanctuaries

they line our backroads
cemetery surrounded
shrines bearing witness

gathering meccas
community citadels
ritual centers

sermon soapboxes
little, white clapboard structures
tiny tin-steepled

ersatz Renaissance
cathedrals of two-by-fours
American kitsch

rural testaments
to weary forlorn faces
seeking salvation

FOMO

In earlier years
I could drift off carefree
wake refreshed
without sense of time lost,
time wasted

Once awareness
of finitude impaled me
that peace was ruptured,
an hour nap became an hour gone
eight hours now eight hours vanished

Sleep no longer a respite,
but a hiatus from life,
a loan from the Reaper
never repayable—
Fear Of Missing Out insomnia

TOP 40 COUNTDOWN

Teenager, 1957, connected to the world!
The transistor radio had arrived,
the size of two sticks of butter,
it fit in my hand, fit in my pocket
a scratchy tinny AM sound,
but music I could carry around,
freed from that monstrous mahogany
Philco that dominated the living room.

Everywhere I went, music was my companion.
I could wear my Blue Suede Shoes
and stay at Elvis' Heartbreak Hotel.
The Hound Dog was now on my leash
so I wouldn't get All Shook Up.
The Platters spun My Prayer
so I could be a Great Pretender.
Along with a Fever from Peggy Lee I could
wonder Who's Sorry Now with Connie Francis
while hoping the Chordettes and Mr. Sandman
would bring me a dream.

I could See You Later Alligator
and Rock Around the Clock with Bill Haley,
Cry along with Johnny Ray
as he was Walking in the Rain.
I could help Tennessee Ernie
shovel those Sixteen Tons,
be on Blueberry Hill with Fats or
in the alley with Little Richard and Long Tall Sally,
I could wonder along with Frankie Lymon
why Fools Fall in Love, I could even
Walk the Line with the man in black.

All this was mine for a couple week's pay
from a part-time job. I could hold my little Sony
close to my ear and the world poured in.
Casey Kasem's Countdown to the Top 40
was a decade away, but two sticks of butter
greased his way onto the airwaves.

Shotgun

"Dibs on shotgun," I'd yell
as we approached Rich's '55 Buick Century.
Shotgun, the front seat of privilege when
cruising the Avenue to impress the chicks,
hard to be cool if stuffed in the back seat.

Remnant from stagecoach days when
the rider in that seat toted the gun,
looked out for trouble, helped navigate,
now the car seat with legroom, better view,
co-pilot duties, control of the AM radio dial.

Back in the '50s, no shotgun rider in
Rich's Buick ever dreamed of carrying
an actual weapon, Pony Express days long gone.
But with road-rage now commonplace, middle fingers
hackneyed, shotgun reclaims some of its old meaning.

X-Rated

Millions of us, crowded,
all only half there, but full of energy
awaiting the cannonade.

Excitement built, explosion imminent,
then jettisoned with the rest,
all seeking to align with an X axis.

Jostling with others I strove to get ahead,
didn't know where I was going, didn't care,
just had to get there, win the race.

Ys of us didn't dare stop and ask directions,
a trait forever ingrained in XYs,
to do so was to lose the race.

Finally, up ahead, the finish line,
in one frantic surge I spurted past others,
broke the barrier, victory was mine.

With a celebratory embrace from an X
I was complete. I remember it all
as if it were 29,000 yesterdays ago.

The American Game

Lessons learned young:
    winning requires financial ruin of others
    destroy or buy out competition
    put houses, hotels on your property
    exploit others through high rents
    Mediterranean, Baltic are worthless immigrant properties
        (ethnic slurs from Park Place, Boardwalk blue-blood
        game-makers)
    you can get out of jail free
    community contributions are penalized
    utilities, transportation should be privately owned
    there are no havens for the homeless, the hungry, the poor

INSIDE MY BOOK'S COVER

You, with your youth, vibrancy, and fresh, toned body—

You see my deeply etched and pain-ridden face,
you see me struggle from my chair, pause for balance,
   limp away,
you see my shriveled hunched posture,
you ask if I need help with my groceries to the car,
you call me "sir,"
you talk to me in sympathetic, even condescending tones,
you see me slowly fold myself into my car,
you see me cautiously drive away.

You, consciously or not, assume all of me is decrepit,
you, who know nothing of aging, presume my mind is also
   crippled.
you know nothing of mature wisdom,
     how chemistry, poetry, experience, books
     have distilled into an elixir of seasoned, seminal
   acumen,
you know nothing of my mind,

never would I trade it for your youthful body.

Nelson Sartoris

BABEL BABBLE

From remnants of Babel
come a thousand tongues,
God, a polyglot, I presume,
speaks, understands every one.

People of all lexicons on earth
declare, swear God talks to them—
yet He does not speak English to me,
only in His science voice is He not mum.

Alternative altars in lab temples
are where I'm able to read His lips,
in reason and logic His mind emerges,
not in babble from multi-tongue pulpits.

Postcard

There's no place like home

Place stamp here

CURIOUS APPELLATION

Why was I saddled with them?
These English/Scandinavian first and middle
given names attached to an Italian surname.

Did the roots lie in Claudius's invasion of Britain
two-thousand years ago? Did Admiral Nelson
have an unknown battle with Garibaldi in the Adriatic?

If so, I might be more accepting. But no, my parents
just wished to name me after my father,
Cornelius Ugo Sartoris. Boy, I dodged a bullet.

There would be no Cornelius, Jr.—Thank you, Lord.
But his moniker was Nello, from there they got Nello's-son;
aka, Nelson. No clue why Edward got in the middle.

Alas, you can't make this stuff up, but of course,
my parents did. Apparently not satisfied,
they named my younger sister, Nella.

The bullet hit her straight on. Any wonder
she uses her middle name, Maria. Maria Sartoris!
The name sings, she should have been an opera star.

Though not entirely displeased with Nelson I'd have
preferred something ethnically consistent: Vittorio or
Leonardo or Vincenzo—and Edoardo, not Edward.

But truth be told, I'd now ditched the whole
Mediterranean thing, and despite its Welsh origin,
opt instead for Tristan. Now there's an epic name—

Tristan Sartoris! Perfect. And besides,
I've been searching for Isolde all my life—
and likely won't find her until death.

All Fixed

An extraordinary day, perhaps a perfect day—
ready to retire, lie flat, read a few pages,
revel in this moment when everything is working,
I start to drift off with a rare sense of peace.

There were no car problems today,
no need to rush to the auto repair shop
or parts store, or put air in the tires,
get it washed, no need to even fill the tank.

No household repairs, malfunctioning appliances,
no furnace or air conditioning breakdowns,
no plumbing problems, no running to hardware stores
in search of a part, no repair men to wait on,

no internet outages, no computer or printer bugs,
no TV cable glitches, no cell phone issues,
garbage disposal, dishwasher worked like a charm,
not even a light bulb needed changing.

Maintenance of modern labor-saving devices
can be very labor intensive. Making life easy
is often difficult, conveniences inconvenient,
repairs a full-time job, but today was Nirvana.

Wait!—What's that noise?
I think I hear the toilet running.

Hanging Out

        once strung

tenement to tenement
        pole to pole
              balcony to balcony

        across America's
alleys
          backyards
                  farmyards

now the rarest
of sights

we strive
to capture solar
and wind power
so we can dry laundry
in clothes dryers

grandma knew
how to air-dry laundry
with wind and sun
years ago

today people air
their dirty laundry
on social media

Mobile Home

Her car almost two decades old. Past collisions evident even in the dark. A taillight taped. Mottled green paint. The gas tank near empty as her purse.

The passenger seat serves as her toddler's room, replete with toys, worn stuffed animals, dirty little blanket, children's books, wooden puzzle pieces. The footwell of the passenger seat serves as pantry—snacks mostly, cookies, potato chips, two cans of tuna, Mountain Dew, a pizza box with a couple cold slices. It also serves as the wastebasket—Happy Meal containers, paper cups, straws, old newspapers, plastic bottles. On the back seat, dirty plaid wool blanket, an old jacket, pillow, sleeping bag, two big black plastic bags, one stuffed with their clothes, the other with assorted items she might pawn.

The day's been spent scrounging for food, scavenging anything of value, panhandling, hunting for toilets, warily talking with others down on their luck—but now it's night.

Seats reclined as blanket, pillow, and sleeping bag are hauled forward. Mother and child burrow beneath them, prepare for another long cold night. She's parked now on a city thoroughfare away from streetlights. City buses thunder by much too close, brakes squealing as they approach the stop ahead.

In the trunk large pieces of cardboard and an old tent—backup plans in case the car gets repossessed—and they are homeless again.

MONDAY JOY

banana peels

                        salmon skins

        burnt toast

                            melon rinds

avocado and peach pits

                        chicken bones

        odors galore

now out at the curb
awaiting the big green truck,
in an instant it's all gone
an empty garbage can—Monday joy!

STUFF

> *The things you own end up owning you.*
> —Brad Pitt, *Fight Club*

stuffed, they've become ubiquitous,
lining highways, rural roads, city streets,
roughly sixty-thousand dot America
three-thousand more each year—still not enough

depositories for our love affair with stuff,
storage shed units shelter worthless overflow
from already overstuffed garages where $800
worth of junk has exiled $100,000 of new
minivans and SUVs to driveways

new on the scene, expensive climate-controlled
storage buildings—they mushroom in number
and size, stuffed with surplus precious fineries

meanwhile, out on tough streets,
homeless wrap themselves for warmth
in cardboard boxes used to ship all this stuff

Summer Symphony

The overture begins with the morning song
of robins, then chickadees, cardinals, finches
join to form a chorus along with
the cacophonic solo of mockingbird banter.

The pace quickens with the symphony's rousing
first movement, featuring timpani reverberations
which escalate with rhythmic back and forth sweeps,
it's the familiar Bach-yard Lawn Mows-art symphony.

An edgy oboe edger leads the lyrical lento
second movement, the whirling of strings
echo the fine finishing touches of a masterpiece
orchestrated by an artistic turf maestro.

In the boisterous third movement scherzo
piercing leaf blowers swirl leaves and blades of grass
into the air with shrill notes of flute and piccolo,
(there's always a blower following the mower).

Highlight of the Rondo Finale is a rollicking
allegro chainsaw slicing and cutting to the core,
the roar of brass and Stihl drums builds to
a crescendo of a falling trunk thump.

Then an unexpected encore, the audience blasted
by Copeland's *Fanfare for the Common Man*,
featuring the trumpet and percussion
staccato of multiple pressure washers.

The crowd exits to robin evening songs,
tomorrow's concert will feature
familiar virtuoso performances by
hedge clippers and car vacuum cleaners.

My Father's Heir Apparent

Once thick, dark, Italian honeyed,
coiffed early in a DA and pompadour,
later a dense crewcut with sideburns,
either way the barber earned his dollar,
copious clippings cascading to the floor,
piles swept away to who knows where.

Early baldness DNA then became the barber,
recessive genes wrought receding hairlines,
accelerated thickness retreat,
honeyed turned to wispy, dark to silver,
now trips to the barber find me
in the twelve items or less aisle.

Water Is Only Good for Washing Your Feet

It's the early fifties, I'm twelve,
unaware it's initiation day.

In Gramps's sub-basement, dug
by his four Italian sons during Prohibition,
the old coal-fired still looms ominously.

Back then the coal pilfered from deep
sunless-day jobs or scrounged discards
on nearby tracks from lumbering trains
bearing the ebony fruit of sweaty scrip labor.

Huddled now on a low bench sit the three of us,
me, Gramps, Dad, known as "Hoocho"
for his delivery role two decades earlier.

Though its days of providing supplemental income
are long gone, the still still works. In a tarnished
metal cup Gramps captures a dram from the trickle,
hands it to me. In broken English he says, *Sip it slow*.

Fire! Fierce! A branding iron! My throat
scorched, my ears fevered. Foreign, very unlike
already customary "dago red" at suppertime.

I emerge from that cellar initiated, one of the men.
Memories of that first sip revived each day at five.

COLLLATERAL DAMAGE

Born in '41 of German and Italian heritage
two languages became forbidden, hidden from me.
Patriotic American kraut and dago kids
would speak only English, as would their parents.
Two languages *tot, morto,* to my world.

Determined to recover my mutter's family tongue,
two years of college German, worst grades of my life.
fehler, besiegt

Thirty years later, determined to speak my padre's patois
while he was still here, a year-long night course
of conversational Italian resulted in year-long public humiliation.
fallimento, sconfitto

With battles lost, war scars remain --
wounded *Zunge,* crippled *lingua*

Sprechen sie Deutsch? Nein, Schcisse
Sai parlare italiano? No, Merda

UNRELATED

All I wanted to do was play ball,
all the time. Stick ball, catch, fast-pitching,
didn't matter. How else could I make
the Cubs and play in Wrigley?

Older brother had other ideas—
Map all different ant colonies
on our Chicago city block, transport
armies of black ants to do battle
with the reds, build mazes to see if they could
locate the sugar cube, watch them bring
the sweet back to their nest and signal
the hoards to come finish the harvest,
excavate anthills to see how deep they went,
experiment with eradication methods,
even electrocution, testing lethal voltage
in his home-made ant electric "chair."
An Orkin man ahead of his time, he bugged me.

No wonder I never played in Wrigley.

SPECIAL DELIVERY

Pablum breadsticks for sibs and me
in divided backseat territories
for the five-hour journey.

Aroma from dozens of fresh-baked
Italian loaves so pervasive it seemed
the old Chevy ran on the vapors.

No wasted crumbs strewn on US 66
south from Chicago to grandparents
in the small coal-mining town of Auburn,

located a hundred miles from anywhere retailing
hard-crusted real bread. So grandparent trips
began at Torino's Bakery in Kensington.

On arrival, hugs from Grandpa would have to wait
'til he first fixed a huge salad from his garden
and with pure ecstasy savored broken-off

pieces of a whole loaf. Then came the hugs.
The world was as good as it would ever get,
manna from the southside of heaven had arrived.

MISCONCEPTION

Things have changed—
my birth day
not as important
as my conception day.

Hard to pin that day down,
subtracting nine months
pegs it at November 2, 1940,
but that's just an estimate,

hardly accurate, No Conception
Certificate, just obsolete Birth one,
so I doubt Social Security will
retro-pay me from that date.

Evidently I'm no longer a Leo,
been reading incorrect horoscopes,
heeding wrong advice for eighty years,
no wonder my life is a mess.

When to light candles now a big question.
My parents should have filed
an amended 1940 return
to include me as a dependent.

Also altered, the day
I could drink legally, vote,
get a driver's license, donate blood,
join the military, buy a gun.

False life-span dates now etched in cemeteries,
yet one thing for sure, we have increased
life expectancy by nine months.
Ah, the marvels of judicial medicine.

Liquid Memories

on a warm day
a cold pilsner his pleasure—
or two, but rarely more

on cool days
a dark ale or stout—
or two, but rarely more

never from a bottle or worse yet, a can—
always from a thin shell glass,
the foamy head admired before sipping

whatever the weather
first swallow the best —
his audible "aahhhh."

dinner time
was for wine—
"dago red" his daily bread

nicknamed "Hoocho"
for prohibition deliveries
of family moonshine

he didn't favor whiskey
except the shot left for Santa
next to carrots for the reindeer

nestled now all snug in my adult bed
I still have visions of him sipping
through fake Santa whiskers

his memory savored every time
a cap or cork is lifted
he's in every swallow

his footsteps I follow
though I can never fill his shoes,
no longer can I fill his glass

just wish he was still here
to share one more—
or two

Fledgling

I thought it hard the first time,
the fledgling when emptying the van
at the college dorm, the long
lonely drive back to the home
where you no longer lived.

Nest emptied, not to be refilled,
the last brood, a page turned
in my book I wasn't finished reading,
the story just getting good,
chapters yet unwritten.

Decades later, void diminished
but the wound not quite healed,
you visit from LA for a few days—
joyous time, house alive, roles changed,
but life complete and whole again.

Then you are winged away in a heartless bird
as I stand there empty, bereft, hollow.
Coming home to barren echoes of joy
that earlier that day filled every corner
I check the flight tracking app on my phone.

I see this little cartoon airplane moving away,
the distance and years between us increasing
once more. When you were born, no one
warned me about this emptiness no one
dared share this, not even in the fine print.

About the Author

Nelson Sartoris earned a PhD in organic chemistry at Northwestern University. For 37 years he was Professor of Chemistry at Wittenberg University in Ohio, where he was the Chair of the Chemistry Department and received the Distinguished Teaching Award. Since retiring and moving to Asheville, NC, in 2005 he has taken courses at the College for Seniors at the Osher Lifelong Learning Institute at the University of North Carolina Asheville. It was there that he began to write poetry. This is his fourth book of collected poems, following *Brain Slivers*, 2016, *On Wings of Words*, 2018, and *With These Hands*, 2020. He lives at Biltmore Lake, NC.

Also available from Pisgah Press & ArsPoetica

Poetry Collections

Letting Go	Donna Lisle Burton
Way Past Time for Reflecting	Donna Lisle Burton
From Roots . . . to Wings	Donna Lisle Burton
This Virgin Page	Jim Carillon
With These Hands	Jim Carillon
And to See Takes Time	Mamie Davis Hilliard
Barricaded Bards: Poems from the Pandemic	The Poets of OLLI
With These Hands	Nelson Sartoris
On Wings of Words	Nelson Sartoris
Brain Slivers	Nelson Sartoris
Invasive Procedures: Earthquakes, Calamities, & poems from the midst of life	Nan Socolow

Fiction

Gabriel's Songbook — Michael Amos Cody
  Finalist, Feathered Quill Book Award, Fiction, 2021

A Twilight Reel — Michael Amos Cody
  Gold Medal, Feathered Quill Book Award, Short Stories, 2021

Trang Sen: A Novel of Vietnam — Sarah-Ann Smith

Mystery

Shade	H. N. Hirsch
Fault Line (coming in 2023)	H. N. Hirsch
The Last of the Swindlers	Peter Loewer
The Rick Ryder Mysteries: Deadly Dancing, Killer Weed, The Pot Professor	RF Wilson

Non-fiction

Letters of the Lost Children: Japan—World War II — Ron Ferster & Jan Atchley Bevan

Musical Morphine: Transforming Pain One Note at a Time — Robin Russell Gaiser
  Finalist, USA Book Awards, 2017

Open for Lunch — Robin Russell Gaiser

Reed's Homophones: A Comprehensive Book of Sound-alike Words — A.D. Reed

Swords in their Hands: George Washington and the Newburgh Conspiracy — Dave Richards
  Finalist, USA Book Awards, History, 2014

Order from online booksellers Amazon or B&N, or from:

Pisgah Press, LLC
PO Box 9663, Asheville, NC 28815
www.pisgahpress.com